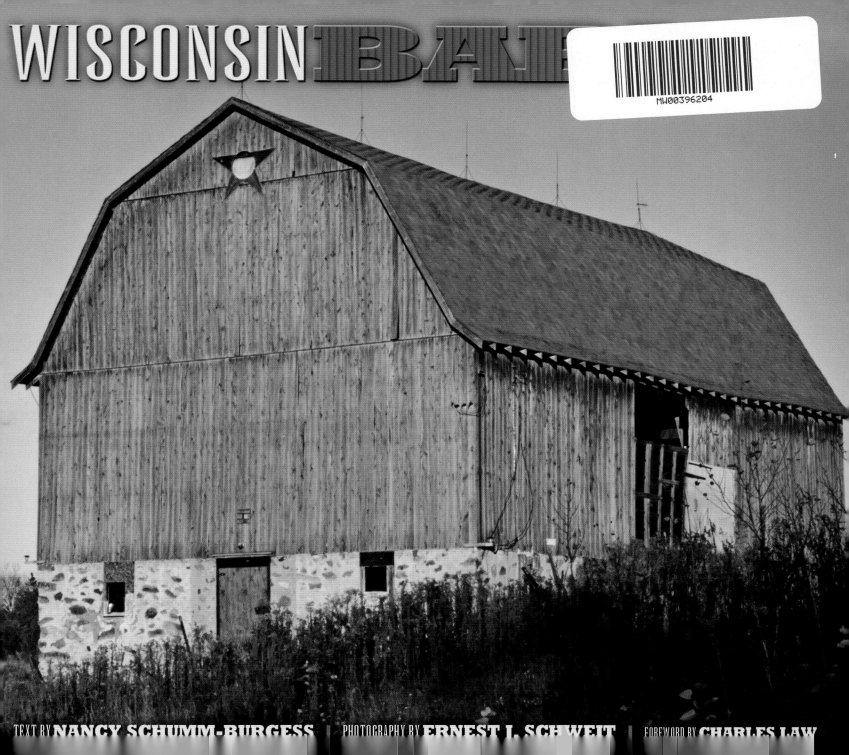

WISCONSIN BARNS

TEXT BY **NANCY SCHUMM-BURGESS** | PHOTOGRAPHY BY **ERNEST J. SCHWEIT** | FOREWORD BY **CHARLES LAW**

COVER: Door County barn in autumn.

COVER, INSETS: See pages 12, 29, 42, 53, and 76.

BACK COVER: Barn along Lake Winnebago near Quinney.

TITLE PAGE: Four of the five points of a star (one of many religious symbols placed on barns) remain on this structure.

FACING PAGE: This barn on a dairy farm in Merrill features a beautiful fieldstone foundation.

This book is dedicated to pioneers, past and present, who continue to intrigue and inspire generations of historians.
—Nancy Schumm-Burgess

To my dad, who planted the seed. My wife, Maureen, who nourished it. And my kids, Jake, Mack, and Sarah, for supporting it.
—Ernest J. Schweit

Special thanks to Bill Koch and Charles Law for their assistance with this book and for their dedication to Wisconsin's history.

ISBN 10: 1-56037-483-7
ISBN 13: 978-1-56037-483-1

© 2009 by Farcountry Press
Photography © 2009 by Ernest J. Schweit
Text © 2009 by Nancy Schumm-Burgess

For more information about our books, write Farcountry Press, P.O. Box 5630, Helena, MT 59604; call (800) 821-3874; or visit www.farcountrypress.com.

Created, produced, and designed in the United States.
Printed in China.

14   13   12   11   10   09   1   2   3   4   5   6

CONTENTS ▌

ABOVE: Simple hardware on the weathered door of a barn built around 1850.

FACING PAGE: This gable-roofed barn in the southern part of the state has been owned by the same family since it was built in the 1880s.

FOREWORD ▌

by Charles Law, Ph.D.
University of Wisconsin–Extension coordinator and one of the founders of the Wisconsin Barn Preservation Program

Wisconsin is blessed with landscapes both varied and breathtaking. If there is one constant, it is the old timber-framed barns that stand stately among forest and cropland. Can you imagine traveling throughout the Wisconsin countryside without seeing these picturesque barns? I can't!

Not only would we be missing what to many has become the officially recognized icon of the state, but we would lose an important connection to the rich array of ethnic groups that settled here and to our agrarian past.

Almost fifteen years ago, I was fortunate to collaborate with several key people in initiating the Wisconsin Barn Preservation Program. It has been the most rewarding part of my career at the University of Wisconsin—because of the people I have met and the amazing stories they have shared.

Through the National Barn Alliance, an organization I led as president for almost six years, I had the added pleasure of meeting many people from around the country who were equally passionate about these buildings. One of those special people was Nancy Schumm-Burgess. And although Nancy comes from the state just south of us, she, too, is passionate about Wisconsin barns and documenting their fascinating histories.

The level of interest in Wisconsin barns never ceases to amaze me. And as this book shows, Wisconsinites love their barns. I have seen barn owners pass around pictures of their barns at preservation workshops much like parents and grandparents do with photographs of their children and grandchildren.

So many of us have grown to appreciate barns not just simply as beautiful buildings, but as important historical records of rural values. As you turn the pages of this book, I hope it helps you develop a similar appreciation.

Read on and enjoy your vicarious visit to many of Wisconsin's barns!

INTRODUCTION

by Nancy Schumm-Burgess

As a passionate barn aficionado living outside Chicago, I often hear the country call my name. It was by such a calling that this search for Wisconsin barns began. I teamed up with Ernie Schweit, a photographer whose passion for barns equals mine, and together we set out on a quest to document these historic structures. We selected Wisconsin, our neighbor to the north, because my family originated in the state and I feel a special kinship to the region.

From the shores of the Mississippi River, Lake Superior, and Lake Michigan to the rough-and-tumble central region, from the graceful prairies and rolling countryside of the south to the dense forests of the north, our barn-hunting quest was like a search for the holy grail. We were certain there were glorious, storied barns out there but wondered if we would find them and, if we did, what condition they would be in. It was all a fabulous adventure in which we seemed to constantly uncover small treasures of history.

Even as urban sprawl creeps out from the state's major cities, Wisconsin's barns still hold the keys to the beauty and history of the state. They unlock a door to the past, shedding light on a simpler time—when connections to family and the land defined American life. The structures demonstrate how much remains the same—and how much has changed.

Farming is still alive in Wisconsin, though there is significant evidence that it is as much in a dramatic state of change as it is in many other parts of the country. With many family farms shifting to large industrial farms, mechanization has replaced manual labor, and children have left the family business for other careers. And as farming has evolved, so has the use of barns. Once the keepers of the important tools of the trade—animals, crops, seed, feed, and equipment—today, many of those same barns are now relegated to glorified storage facilities, or worse, white elephants. By documenting them, we sought to preserve the memory of the structures and the way of life they represent, before they would be lost to time and the elements.

For the purposes of this book, we chose to divide the state into five regions: the Northwoods and Lake Superior to the north; Central Wisconsin in the heart of the state; the Mississippi River Valley to the southwest; Lake Michigan to the east; and the Prairie and Kettle region to the southeast.

As we got to know these barns of Wisconsin, we uncovered a treasure trove of variety in which regional styles emerged. Barn architecture seemed to reflect the challenges faced in each region. In Central Wisconsin, in the Mississippi River Valley, and in the Prairie and Kettle region, where there were vast tracts of cropland, larger structures for storage and machinery were needed to support the operations. In the Northwoods and along Lake Michigan, where the farms were mostly for family use, the structures were more modest in size.

With the help of Bill Koch, rock expert extraordinaire, we were able to make connections between the materials used in foundations and the geological history of the regions. When we traveled to the Northwoods and Lake Superior area, we discovered barn foundations made of locally quarried black granite; in the Mississippi River Valley, limestone provided the foundation stones.

In Central Wisconsin, we found barns built from local tamarack trees, with rough-hewn logs still supporting the main framework, as well as more modern, though still traditionally styled barns of today's Amish. We toured the traditional barns of the German and Scandinavian pioneers in the Northwoods area. As a bonus, we discovered the "fad barns" of the early twentieth century:

the round barns and the equilateral arch barns that were popular in pockets throughout the state.

On a quest such as ours, it was important to have a flare for adventure—and no fear. Leaving our respective homes in Illinois and driving countless miles on country roads that were often not included on our battered map was a bit daunting. But the rewards were plenty. Around each corner, no matter the time of year, we witnessed awe-inspiring vistas. In the Northwoods, we saw endless miles of thick forest, broken by similar miles of lakes—less than ideal conditions for farming, yet several were carved out amid the rocky terrain. Along the Great Lakes, we saw farmsteads situated on sandy roadways a short distance from the shores of Lake Michigan. Along the Mississippi River Valley, we visited farms nestled within deep valleys overlooking the great river. Central Wisconsin featured riverside mills and barns set with rocky backdrops and steep, tree-covered hills. In some parts of the state, the terrain changed suddenly from one extreme to the other, with vast expanses of prairie suddenly shifting to captivating river bottom. As a bonus to the barns, we saw glacial ravines, river headwaters, and the sacred tribal ground belonging to the Potawatomi Indians.

As we sought to capture these beloved barns in images and words, we realized we could never adequately convey the sounds and sensations of the tranquil farms. Country life has its own soundtrack: the gentle rustle of wind through the grasslands; the distant call of a hawk hunting over a broad prairie; the sharp melodies of songbirds in the forests. There is also, most importantly, a lack of sound: the hushed silence of snowy winter days in the country—a palpable absence of traffic, construction equipment, and airplanes.

Over the course of the two years it took to complete this project, the weather played an important role in the process of documenting the state's historic barns. Whether in color-infused fall or in frigid winter, that notorious Wisconsin weather introduced us to some remarkable people and created dramatic backdrops for Ernie's beautiful photographs. Some of our favorite structures were nestled in the pine and birch woods of Central Wisconsin, and we photographed them during the peak of the autumn hues. We traveled through sub-zero temperatures and white-out conditions, managing to navigate icy roadways covered with a thin blanket of snow that masked the slick pavement underneath. Strangers welcomed us into their homes as we sought to escape the treacherous conditions. As our journey drew to a close in the summer, we were thankful for the warm food and cold beers that awaited us in regional hotels and restaurants or in the cottage of a friend.

By the end of our quest through Wisconsin, we had met Packer fans, large families, small families, Amish families, renters, and ex-pats from Chicago, as well as the ancestors of early settlers who still carried on their family traditions. We had purchased fresh produce, and we had been tempted by the furnishings built by the hands of a skilled carpenter. We had listened as one man shared the beauty of his reconstructed round barn; many others had told us how much they appreciated the historical nature of their barns, even as they were challenged to keep up the maintenance.

The barns that remain in this state tell a clear story about farming, past and present. Our hope is that through our book, readers will understand this story of hard work, of hopes and dreams—both realized and lost. These barns represent what the settlers, dreamers, and hard-working families found at the end of their own quests.

THE NORTHWOODS AND LAKE SUPERIOR

Occupying the northern third of Wisconsin along Lake Superior, the Northwoods region is characterized by dense forests of pine, birch, and maple trees and acres of finger-like lakes. Powerful glaciers carved this landscape thousands of years ago, scraping the surface clean of glacial till and leaving behind only large boulders and rocky outcrops.

This region is not exactly farming country, with its rough landscape, harsh northern winters, and short growing season. Its history is tied more to the logging and mining industries, which thrived in the late nineteenth century. The farms that do exist here were built on rare pockets of rich soil that were not plowed away by ancient glaciers. Some of these unexpected farmsteads are perched on expansive hilltops overlooking long valleys; others are nestled in the woodlands adjacent to large tracts of open land.

Barns in this region reflect the souls of the hearty. The sturdy stone foundations and wooden structures seem to symbolize the resilient spirit of the families who settled the area. There are historic log structures built by the early lumberers and mining families, barns with elaborate stone foundations, and uniquely designed structures used as smokehouses. Mixed in with the old gable- and gambrel-roofed barns are some modern buildings, such as the arch-roofed barns of the early and mid-twentieth century.

The deep history in the Northwoods is matched only by the depths of its expansive hardwood forests. To wander amid its historic farms and hear the whisper of their tales is an unforgettable experience.

LEFT, TOP: What resembles a lighthouse is actually a silo next to a small smokehouse built of locally quarried stone.

LEFT: This barn is adorned with hex signs, which in the late nineteenth century were believed to keep away evil spirits.

ABOVE: The peak of an arch-roofed barn near Amery appears above a snowy horizon. A variety of arch-roofed barns can be seen in the Northwoods. The style, which emerged in the early twentieth century as a result of declining availability of lumber due to World War I, is sometimes called an "equilateral" or "rainbow roof" barn. This barn style was particularly popular on dairy farms.

ABOVE: Poised on the edge of rolling countryside—beautiful, even in the dreary days of winter—this farm represents several generations of tough farmers in Wisconsin. The wooden barns were built around 1929 using the remnants of a large tannery in Montreal, Wisconsin, a historic mining town along the Canadian border. Legend has it that the farm was originally the site of a productive gold mine.

ABOVE: Built in the mid-1900s, this arch-roofed barn in the lakes region served a small family with simple needs. The lower level boasted a milking parlor and storage for a horse or two, while the lofts provided plenty of winter storage for hay.

ABOVE, TOP: Located along Potato Lake in northern Wisconsin, this simple structure was used for a variety of purposes during its lifetime, including boat storage, ice storage, fish sorting, and animal breeding.

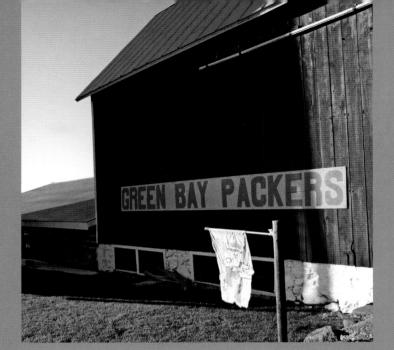

ABOVE: The Pennsylvania Dutch were among the first to decorate the sides of their barns, often with hex signs. Today, the tradition continues, though the Packers fans certainly do not mean it as a hex *(above, top)*. A similar tradition of advertising on barns dates back to the early 1900s, when Americans began traveling by automobile *(above)*.

LEFT: Once the hay is cut and baled, a conveyor carries the bales up to the lofts, where they are stored.

LEFT, TOP: Built of rough-hewn logs, this rare barn dates to the 1840s, when Wisconsin's first timber workers came to the state from as far away as Scandinavia. Families working for the Montreal Mining Company—at one time one of the world's deepest iron mines—later used the barn.

LEFT: Ever notice how most old barns are red? In the early days of farming, people used linseed oil, an orange-colored oil from the seeds of the flax plant, to seal the wood on their barns. They would also often mix in milk, lime, and lye, as well as ferrous oxide, or rust, which enhanced the orange-red color.

BELOW: Only faint hints of paint linger on this once snow-white barn.

FACING PAGE: Access to a consistent source of water was, and is, essential to a viable farm. This one is ideally located along the Flambeau River.

I INE CR ST FARM

ABOVE: Pictured here in winter's grip, a barn on the Pine Crest Farm awaits spring's return. Note its beautiful arch roof and matching side doors.

FACING PAGE, TOP: The first upright wooden silo was constructed in McHenry County, Illinois, in 1873. This log silo mimics that early design. Over time, wooden silos proved impractical and were replaced by concrete or brick structures in the early 1900s, which were then followed by a shift to steel in the mid-1900s.

FACING PAGE, BOTTOM LEFT: An old tractor seat serves as a charming, rustic adornment.

FACING PAGE, BOTTOM RIGHT: A hay conveyor, which moves baled hay in and out of the barn as needed, allows slivers of cold to access the interior, while the rest of the barn remains locked up tight.

ABOVE: Like barns on the plains, this structure was designed with a somewhat low, sloped profile to withstand winds. The framework combines old post-and-beam construction with mortise-and-tenon joints. Once a horse barn, today the building is used for special events.

RIGHT: This now-weathered barn door faithfully kept the elements out and the animals in.

FACING PAGE: The stones in the foundation of this barn fit together like puzzle pieces. Foundations had to be solid in order to support the thousands of pounds of wood framing.

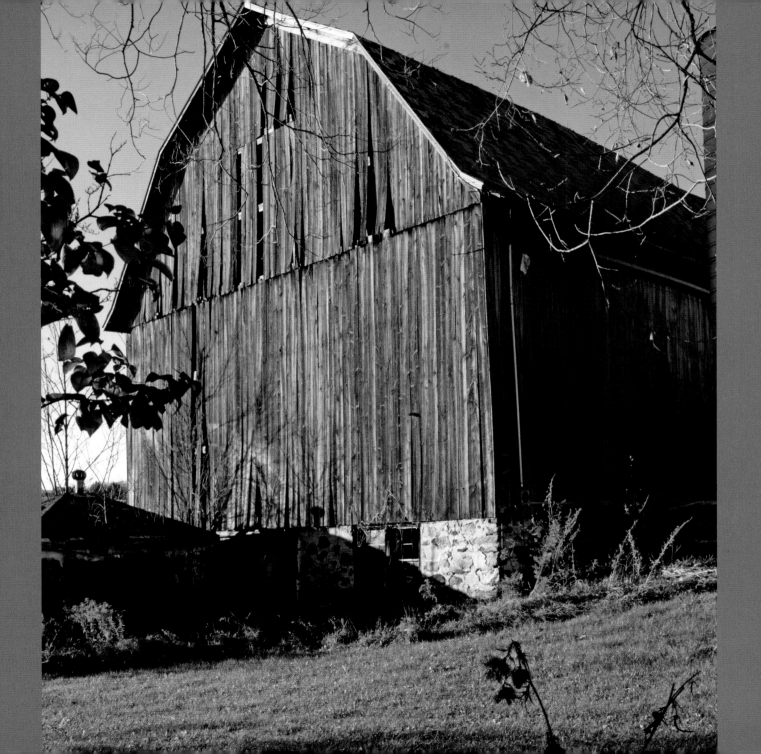

ABOVE: Two curious cows mosey up to the fence for a closer look at the photographer. A carpenter built this barn in the 1920s for his family operation. The family consisted of eleven children—ages nine months to eighteen years—when the mother passed away. The family's tragic story became local legend because they were able to survive in the farming business for another generation, without their mother.

FACING PAGE: Located near Lake Superior, this barn was built around 1900. At the turn of the nineteenth century, barns had reached their peak in size. They were multi-use structures—with everything important to the function of the farm stored in one place—as opposed to singular in purpose. Barn builder Rick Bott says that a farm with a very large barn and modest home truly had its priorities in order in 1900.

ABOVE: Early morning light finds the family horses grazing on a ranch near Merrill.

FACING PAGE: A wintry scene west of Pine River. The tradition of building the barn away from the house is an early American one, a practice particularly popular in the Midwest. This gable-roofed barn, which dates to the mid-1800s, was built in a style popularized by early English American settlers, who called them "wheat barns."

CENTRAL WISCONSIN ▮

Nestled between lush woodlands to the north, rolling countryside to the west, broad prairies to the south, and Lake Michigan to the east is varied and picturesque Central Wisconsin. Here, ancient glaciers carved their routes through the landscape, leaving behind rocky ridges and deep gorges. They deposited glacial debris as they made their slow, powerful move southwest, laying a foundation of rich soil for future farming.

In the early days of settlement, this fertile land attracted a flood of pioneers from the East. The majority came from New York, finding the terrain and climate of Wisconsin similar to their home state. These settlers chose well, as Central Wisconsin would prove to have the finest conditions for farming: a wealth of hardwood trees for use in constructing homes and barns, abundant water sources, and the richest soil in the state.

The region is home to the largest number of historic barns in the state, many beautifully situated, well kept, and easily accessible. Most are relics of early dairy farming, an industry that has dominated Wisconsin since the late nineteenth century. Very few wheat barns remain from the mid-nineteenth century, when wheat was the king crop in the state—until a small bug referred to as the "chinch bug" nearly wiped out Wisconsin's wheat crop.

An examination of barn foundations reveals locally quarried granite, another gift left behind by the ancient glaciers. Atop these unique foundations are structures crafted of local tamarack, oak, and walnut.

We found a common thread among the owners of these historic structures: the passionate belief that the barns are a critical tie to the history of the communities and the state. As we visited these warm and friendly families who were more than eager to stop what they were doing to share family stories and give tours, we knew they were right.

ABOVE: The foundation of this early 1900s barn is made of sandstone that was removed from nearby cliffs and hauled to the site. The gambrel roof utilizes a "balloon frame," which eliminated much of the cross-framing and opens up more of the central lofts for hay storage.

FACING PAGE: Looking into the window of an old milking parlor.

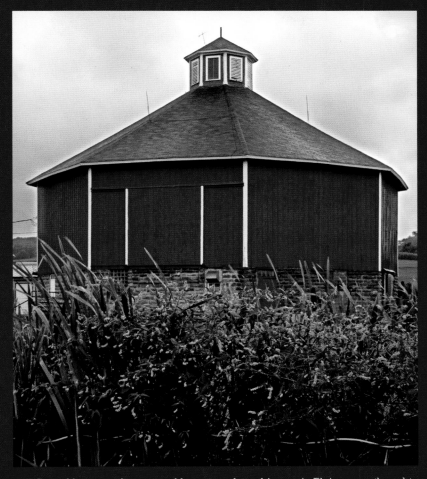

ABOVE: Round barns and octagonal barns, such as this one in Plain, were thought to offer a more efficient use of interior space. The silo was often placed in the center and was capped by a cupola, which improved circulation throughout the barn by allowing heat to escape.

LEFT: This pastoral scene near Wausau is a classic example of a traditional early-twentieth-century family farm. A barn "kit" could be ordered through companies such as Louden and Gordon Machine, and Sears, Roebuck. The affordable kits arrived with instructions, wood, and hardware that allowed the farmer and local workers to construct the entire structure on site.

RIGHT, TOP AND BOTTOM: These century-old barns brace against the elements and time. Note the doors on the sides of each barn. These doors accessed the main threshing floors, and they would be opened to allow the wind to blow through the barns, thus clearing away the chaff from the wheat. These doorways had a band of wood at the entry, called a threshold, that kept the wheat from blowing away as well.

BELOW: Ghostlike, two horses pause beside a barn in Pittsville.

ABOVE, LEFT AND RIGHT: Sometimes it's the details that define country living: barn kittens warming themselves in the sun and an old water pump and bucket.

FACING PAGE: By the mid-twentieth century, many traditional barns had been replaced by pole barns. Constructed of aluminum siding on a simple wooden framework, pole barns are less expensive and easier to construct.

ABOVE: A barn and windmill look out over a rolling field of corn in the late spring. Windmills harnessed the power of the wind to pump water out of the ground.

FACING PAGE, TOP: Birch trees in fall finery guide the eye to this old barn nestled along a back road in Marathon County.

FACING PAGE, BOTTOM: A vigorous corn crop seems to thwart this barn's advertising.

ABOVE: This octagonal barn is located on a thriving Holstein farm in La Valle. Registered Holsteins are raised solely for dairy production and are known for their large milk yields.

FACING PAGE: The long tradition of dairy farming continues in central Wisconsin. The state has the largest number of milk-producing cows in the nation.

ABOVE, LEFT: An old carriage wheel near Fennimore.

ABOVE, RIGHT: A window allows a glimpse into the soul of this board-and-batten-sided barn.

ABOVE, TOP: The weathered siding on this old gambrel-roofed barn protects the remaining framework.

FACING PAGE: Builders tilted the window at the top of this barn in order to place it as high as possible. Windows such as this were the only light source in hay lofts.

THE MISSISSIPPI RIVER VALLEY

Serving as the western boundary of the state, the Mississippi River Valley is characterized by beautiful pastoral settings amid verdant, rolling countryside. Unlike much of Wisconsin's topography, this valley was devoid of glacial activity; glaciers were diverted south and west to today's Illinois and Iowa, respectively. This valley is referred to as Wisconsin's "driftless area," a region that would prove to have mineral-rich soil that allowed the farming industry to flourish.

The Mississippi River served as an important resource for the region, providing transportation for goods and people. Settlers on farmsteads used the Mississippi to sell produce to broader markets. River towns sprang up, serving as vital crossing areas for the overland trails that guided eager settlers to the promised land of the West.

Settlers from England were among the first to build homes and farmsteads in the Mississippi River Valley, particularly in the southern reaches of the state. Evidence of these early settlers remains today in the form of traditional English wheat barns. Several farmsteads are home to multiple generations of barn styles that span nearly a century of architecture. The structures of this region reflect the variety of cultural influences, from Amish settlers to cheese producers from Switzerland.

Visiting these barns is like moving through time, experiencing a history as rich as Mississippi River Valley soil. Much of this history lives on in the people who cherish these barns and in the farming lifestyle they continue to embrace.

ABOVE: One of the most photographed sites in Wisconsin, the Dells Mill in Augusta dates to 1864.

FACING PAGE: This dairy farm looks out over the Mississippi River from its perch atop a hillside.

ABOVE: Magazines such as the *Prairie Farmer* published articles on how to
build structures to house different animals. This structure once served as
a small chicken coop and was later modified to store farm equipment.

FACING PAGE: Round barns began to appear in the Midwest in the early 1900s.
Vernon Township, Wisconsin, has a particularly large number of them.
This one was constructed by African American architect Algie Shivers,
a local carpenter, who specialized in this trendy style.

ABOVE: Arch-roofed barns vary, but most were designed to have completely open upper lofts for maximum hay storage.

ABOVE, RIGHT: This arch-roofed barn near Glenwood City once housed a large dairy herd. The pitch of the roof indicates the lofts could hold many tons of hay to feed the cows in the milking parlor below.

LEFT: A forest of leafless trees surrounds this century-old red barn with a gambrel roof; it has seen many winters in the small town of Spring Valley.

ABOVE: Snow blankets this working farm in Monroe County. Winter doesn't mean the end of farm work; it just shifts indoors. The mural depicts migrating geese that head south before winter hits but return to Wisconsin each spring.

FACING PAGE: Bales of hay dot a snow-covered field in Spring Valley.

ABOVE: When the walls begin to collapse and the roof is giving way, humor is a good way to deal with the impending crumble.

LEFT: Southwestern Wisconsin is home to several Amish settlements, including this one near Cashton. Amish families have long emigrated from Pennsylvania to Wisconsin's rolling countryside to continue their farming traditions of centuries past.

ABOVE: A small dairy barn and attached chicken coop in St. Croix County.

RIGHT: Though no longer active, this mill and dam south of Merrillan endure another frigid winter. Despite the mill's cracked foundation, it remains as a symbol of Wisconsin's early hydroelectric technology.

ABOVE: Some farms hold curious collections of old buildings, like this small home in Trempealeau that dates back to the 1840s. It once served as a servants quarters. The gambrel-roofed barn next to it dates to the early 1900s. This Mississippi River Valley farm is not far from where legendary 1920s gangster Al Capone allegedly did a lot of business during Prohibition, producing illegal liquor in hiding places in the area's hillsides and using the Mississippi to transport it around the country.

FACING PAGE: The extension of the roof on this barn served to protect and shade the man who stood at the door and guided hay into the upper lofts as it was transported from ground level by a hay conveyor.

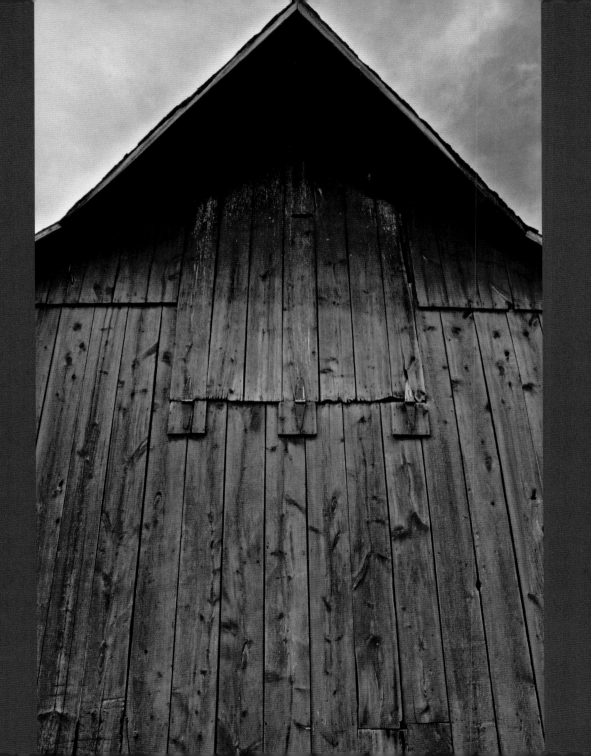

ABOVE: The skeleton of an old, wooden barn door, grayed with age.

FACING PAGE: Completed on July 13, 1876, by the current owner's great grandfather, this barn stands strong in a field of soybeans west of Green Bay. Note the classic gabled roof, German-style banked north side, stone foundation, and early silo.

LAKE MICHIGAN

Eastern Wisconsin is fronted by miles of Lake Michigan and Green Bay shoreline, which have long provided ports for the transportation of goods to and from the region. The sandy soils pushed traditional farming inland, but the nearby ports provided venues for selling produce.

Although Door County is now a tourist destination, historically it was home to shipbuilders and farmers. The early farms of this region were mostly small family operations serving the needs of the maritime community. Produce such as grapes and cherries became the stock and trade of Door County. The barns were built from locally quarried stones and lumber. Most of these simple, practical structures have succumbed to weather and time, yet their moss-covered foundations and the beautiful patina of their aged siding convey a great deal of character.

In contrast, the historic barns that still stand along Lake Michigan and Green Bay are larger, multi-generational barns. Most were constructed around the turn of the nineteenth century and reflect the classic multipurpose barns of that era. They have gabled or gambrel roofs, foundations of locally quarried stone, and large areas for storing the family's farming tools and equipment.

These family barns serve as reminders of rural life as small port towns grow into large cities and farms give way to industry. The modest and charming structures, and the remarkable people who protect and maintain them, are keepers of keys to Wisconsin's storied past.

ABOVE: A pleasing mix of textures in Door County.

ABOVE, LEFT: Tradition is the cornerstone of family farming. The builders of this barn, near the headwaters of the Milwaukee River, etched in stone the date of its construction and an image of a horse. Some builders carved their names in the beams of barns.

FACING PAGE: Returning from the fields in New London.

ABOVE: Almost everything on a farm can be recycled and re-purposed, from milk pails to wooden crates.

FACING PAGE: A log snake-rail fence winds around historic structures in Door County. The buildings, which date to the mid-nineteenth century, housed the small farm's animals, feed, and firewood. The lightning rods atop the structures date to the end of the nineteenth century. Each rod features a hand-blown glass ornament that helps to diffuse electrical current if the rod is struck. These rods were all that kept these wooden structures from going up in flames from a lightning-sparked fire.

ABOVE: Silos were built of various materials, from wood to rock, with varying degrees of success. This turn-of-the-nineteenth-century silo was made by pouring concrete in segments, starting at ground level and working to the top, a practice that began in the late 1800s. Considering that the first silo was built in 1873, advances in their construction progressed rapidly. Note the conical top; this was one of the earlier styles for silo caps.

ABOVE: Early German farmers were experts at clearing fields of stones and constructing sturdy buildings that have held up over many decades.

FACING PAGE: A proud old barn in Door County stands amid fall color, ready to weather another winter.

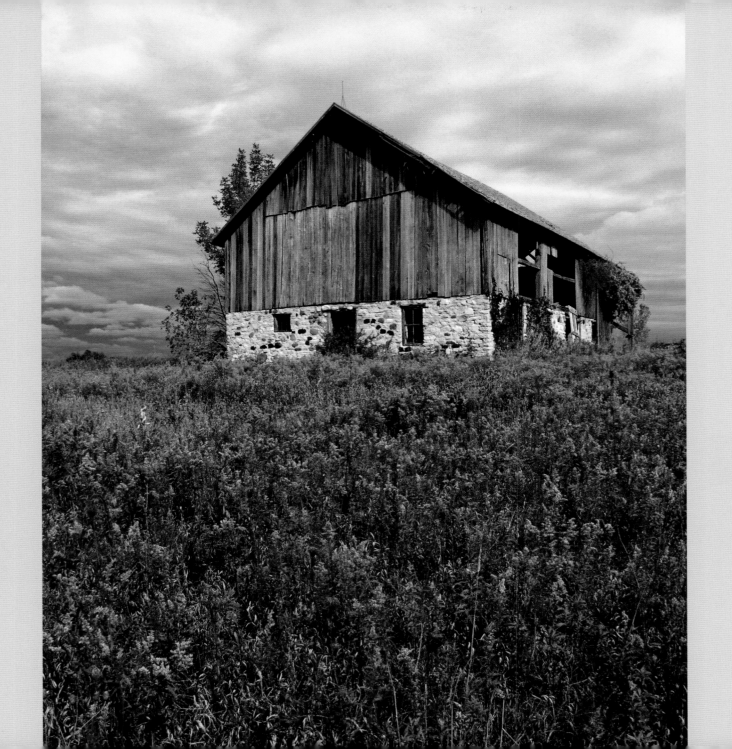

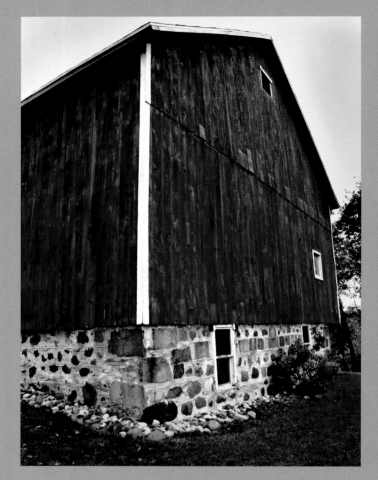

ABOVE: A single Virginia creeper vine climbs up a dolomite limestone foundation.

ABOVE, LEFT: The careful and decorative placing of the shale in this red barn's foundation demonstrates the pride that the barn builder took in his artistry.

FACING PAGE: Nature and the elements reclaim a roadside barn east of Lomira.

ABOVE: Grape vines overtake an old fence encircling a mill along the headwaters of the Milwaukee River. Historically, mills provided a place to grind grain, mill lumber, and swap stories with other locals.

FACING PAGE: This farmer in Door County plows the field on a cool spring day, in the time-honored tradition of preparing a field for seeding.

PRAIRIE AND KETTLE

This beautiful region in southeastern Wisconsin is characterized by vast expanses of prairie dotted with ancient glacial landforms called kettles. These pits formed when partially buried masses of glacial ice melted, leaving behind depressions in the ground.

The glaciers also left behind rich soils ideal for farming. Indeed, this region boasted some of the best conditions for farming in the state: flat, well-drained soils; plenty of fresh water; and enough timber for constructing fences and structures but not so much that it overtook potential farmland. Dairy farming has been so successful in this region that Wisconsin remains one of the nation's top dairy producers.

The majority of the barns remaining in this region today stand on what were once large family farms. Most are post–Civil War era structures built specifically for dairy farming. These historic barns have the intricate stone foundations and the large post-and-beam framework of the late nineteenth century. They served multiple purposes, housing everything in one structure: livestock in the lower level; equipment, grain, and feed in the central threshing floor; and hay in the upper lofts. Many of these solidly constructed late-1800s structures were used for their original purposes well into the late 1900s.

Most of these beautiful edifices were built during neighborhood barn raisings, in which communities joined together to help new neighbors begin their farming operations. First a "barn architect" would design the family barn. Then family and laborers would prepare the beams, and the community would gather to raise the barn. In their traditional roles, men and boys worked on the structures and the women prepared food for the workers and helped the family settle in.

The size and magnitude of these structures is synonymous with the families' values and traditions. The glorious barns of this region are Wisconsin's prairie castles and, like many barns in the Midwest, have come to symbolize Americana.

ABOVE: In the late 1800s traveling salesmen wandered through farm country selling hardware, such as steel hinges.

LEFT: There were many stagecoach stops along the route between Madison and Milwaukee in the late nineteenth century. This farmstead in Sullivan is rumored to have been such a stop.

ABOVE, LEFT AND RIGHT: Contrasting foundations—one stone, one large brick—are both so precise as to require no mortar.

RIGHT: Hay bales await pick-up near a small red barn sitting beneath an expansive sky. Author John Madsen describes the region's tallgrass prairie as the land "where the sky began."

ABOVE: This large arch-roofed barn in Bristol features an enormous milking parlor nearly 100 feet in length. This farm was once a large provider of dairy products for Wisconsin and the greater region.

RIGHT: The grass has been cut, dried, and baled, while the corn continues to grow.

FACING PAGE: Thistle plants frame this view of a dairy farm in Racine County. Scenes like this make it clear why these historic structures are called prairie castles. The barn was built in two sections, with a classic gambrel roof on the right and a Dutch gambrel roof on the left. This newer addition on the left was added as the business grew. The number of silos indicates this dairy herd was a large one; silos store the cows' feed, called silage, which consists of corn stalks that are chopped and allowed to ferment.

ABOVE: From 1797 to 1845 nurseryman John Chapman traveled throughout the Midwest passing out apple seeds and small apple trees to settlers. The generous man who introduced apples to the region became known as Johnny Appleseed. It is estimated that all trees west of Ohio originated from his nursery stock. Families made applesauce, apple butter, apple cakes, apple wine, apple vinegar, canned apples, apple dumplings, and apple cider from this new fruit.

FACING PAGE: The siding on this gable-roofed barn near Sullivan allows a glimpse of its framework.

ABOVE, LEFT: Rolled hay bales that shed water replaced the traditional squared bales in the late twentieth century, and large barns built to accommodate the storage of squared bales began to disappear.

ABOVE, CENTER AND RIGHT: The brick silo with the cone top (*center*) was a trial style of silo in the late 1800s. The dome-topped silo (*right*) dates to the early 1900s. Silos of this style were replaced by the blue steel Harvestore silos, which were introduced at the Wisconsin State Fair in 1948.

FACING PAGE: A large, century-old barn stands on the edge of a wide expanse of prairie near Bristol.

ABOVE: Exhibiting venting and an elaborate roofline, this unique structure south of Portage either served as a granary or was used as a barn for horses and carriages. The tiled silo behind it is an example of an experimental style from the early 1900s.

FACING PAGE: Morning fog lifts, revealing an arch-roofed barn, silo, and freshly seeded field in the southeastern corner of the state.

Silhouetted against a pastel sunset,
this historic barn in Cleveland stands
as a proud reminder of Wisconsin's rich
agrarian past and the hope for its future.

ABOUT THE AUTHORS

An avid history writer, **Nancy Schumm-Burgess** has been documenting and preserving barns since 1997. She works with local and national barn preservation organizations to protect this integral part of our agrarian heritage. Schumm-Burgess is the author of *Images of America: Long Grove; The Barns of Lake County; Hearts Full of Compassion; Gardens and Other Sanctuaries in Long Grove, Illinois;* and many history articles for regional publications. Schumm-Burgess serves as director of a land trust.

Ernest J. Schweit fell in love with rural America from the window of a train he rode to college in downstate Illinois. He saw a lonely beauty in the barns and farmhouses that would become his passion and favorite photographic subject. Schweit lives outside Chicago with his artist wife, three children, dog, and cat. www.mfisherstudios.com

BIBLIOGRAPHY

Austin, Russell H. *The Wisconsin Story.* Milwaukee, Wisconsin: *Milwaukee Journal,* 1969.

Crowns, Byron. *Wisconsin Through 5 Billion Years of Change.* Wisconsin Earth Sciences Center, 1976.

Current, Richard Nelson. *Wisconsin, A History.* Champaign: University of Illinois Press, 2001.

Dott, Robert H., Jr., and John W. Attig. *Roadside Geology of Wisconsin.* Missoula, Montana: Mountain Press Publishing Company, 2004.

Madsen, John. *Where the Sky Began: Land of the Tallgrass Prairie.* Iowa City: University of Iowa Press, 1995.

Pukite, John. *A Field Guide to Cows.* New York: Penguin Books, 1996.

Schumm-Burgess, Nancy. *The Barns of Lake County.* Marceline, Missouri: Donning Company Publishers, 2004.

Simmonds, William. *Advertising Barns.* St. Paul, Minnesota: Motor Books International, 2004.